T0402764

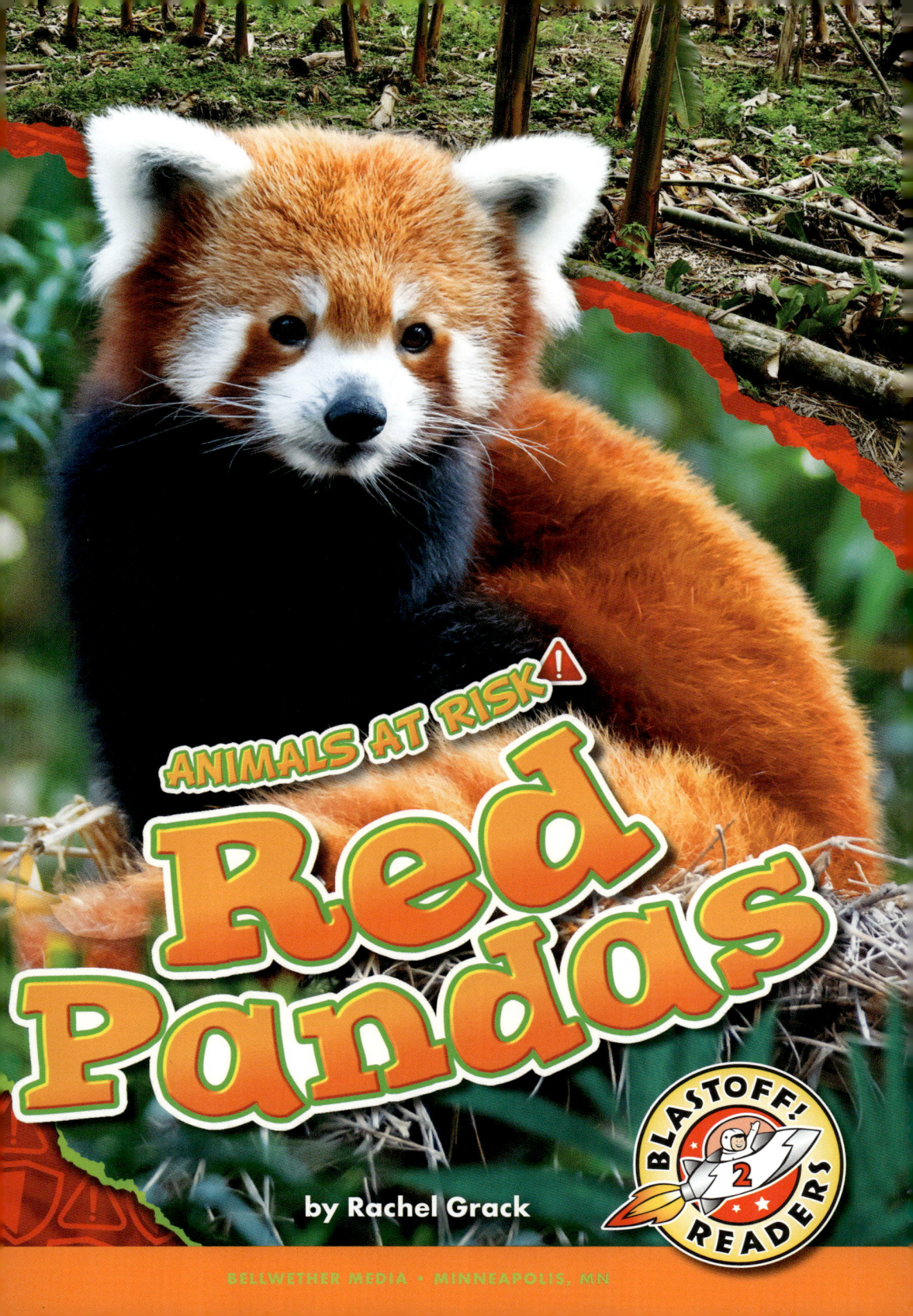

ANIMALS AT RISK ⚠️

Red Pandas

by Rachel Grack

BLASTOFF!
2
READERS

BELLWETHER MEDIA • MINNEAPOLIS, MN

Blastoff! Readers are carefully developed by literacy experts to build reading stamina and move students toward fluency by combining standards-based content with developmentally appropriate text.

Level 1 provides the most support through repetition of high-frequency words, light text, predictable sentence patterns, and strong visual support.

Level 2 offers early readers a bit more challenge through varied sentences, increased text load, and text-supportive special features.

Level 3 advances early-fluent readers toward fluency through increased text load, less reliance on photos, advancing concepts, longer sentences, and more complex special features.

LEVELS

★ **Blastoff! Universe**

Reading Level

Grade **K**

Grades **1–3**

Grade **4**

This edition first published in 2024 by Bellwether Media, Inc.

No part of this publication may be reproduced in whole or in part without written permission of the publisher. For information regarding permission, write to Bellwether Media. Inc., Attention: Permissions Department, 6012 Blue Circle Drive, Minnetonka, MN 55343.

Library of Congress Cataloging-in-Publication Data

Names: Koestler-Grack, Rachel A., 1973- author.
Title: Red pandas / Rachel Grack.
Description: Minneapolis, MN : Bellwether Media, 2024. | Series: Blastoff! Readers. Animals at risk | Includes bibliographical references and index. | Audience: Ages 5-8 | Audience: Grades 2-3 | Summary: "Relevant images match informative text in this introduction to why red pandas are at risk. Intended for students in kindergarten through third grade"-- Provided by publisher.
Identifiers: LCCN 2023004262 (print) | LCCN 2023004263 (ebook) | ISBN 9798886874228 (library binding) | ISBN 9798886876109 (ebook)
Subjects: LCSH: Red panda--Juvenile literature. | Red panda--Conservation--Juvenile literature.
Classification: LCC QL737.C214 K64 2024 (print) | LCC QL737.C214 (ebook) | DDC 599.76/3--dc23/eng/20230130
LC record available at https://lccn.loc.gov/2023004262
LC ebook record available at https://lccn.loc.gov/2023004263

Editor: Kieran Downs   Designer: Brittany McIntosh

Printed in the United States of America, North Mankato, MN.

Table of Contents

Forest Climbers

Red pandas are small, furry **mammals**. They have dark red markings on their faces.

There are two **species** of red pandas. They live in mountain forests in southern Asia.

5

bamboo

Red pandas mostly eat bamboo. It grows on certain parts of mountains.

6

But people are destroying red panda **habitats**. Today, the animals are **endangered**.

Red Panda Range

N
W E
S

range =

7

logging

Red pandas once had wide **home ranges**. But people cleared bamboo forests for logging, farms, and firewood.

Poachers kill red pandas. They sell red panda furs.

1

people
need farms

2

bamboo forests
are cleared

3

red pandas lose
food and homes

Red pandas have trouble finding enough food. **Livestock** eat and destroy bamboo.

Bamboo needs the right weather to grow. But **climate change** brings warmer weather. Bamboo cannot grow.

livestock

10

Red Panda Stats

Least Concern	Near Threatened	Vulnerable	Endangered	Critically Endangered	Extinct in the Wild	Extinct

conservation status: endangered

life span: up to 14 years

Save the Red Pandas!

Red pandas are important for their mountain **ecosystems**.

They keep bamboo from overgrowing. This helps other forest plants stay healthy.

The World with Red Pandas

1 more red pandas → 2 healthy bamboo growth

3 healthy forests

Governments **protect** red panda habitats. They set up **reserves** for red pandas.

red panda in a reserve

Wildlife groups make pathways
to connect red panda homes.

Governments pass **laws** that make it illegal to hunt red pandas.

16

People become forest guardians. They patrol bamboo forests and stop poachers.

17

Wildlife workers teach communities about red pandas.

wildlife workers

18

yak poop
used for fires

Farmers learn new ways to plant crops and **herd** animals. People can burn yak poop to make fires instead of bamboo.

Walking or riding bikes instead of driving slows climate change.

Adopting a red panda is another way to help. Together, everyone can save red pandas!

Glossary

adopting—taking over the care for someone or something; people who adopt wild animals give money for someone else to care for them.

climate change—a human-caused change in Earth's weather due to warming temperatures

ecosystems—communities of plants and animals living in certain places

endangered—in danger of dying out

habitats—places and natural surroundings in which plants or animals live

herd—to keep or look after farm animals

home ranges—lands on which animals or groups of animals live, hunt, and travel

laws—rules that must be followed

livestock—animals raised on a farm, such as goats, sheep, and cows

mammals—warm-blooded animals that have backbones and feed their young milk

poachers—hunters who catch or harm animals illegally

protect—to keep safe

reserves—lands set aside for wildlife

species—kinds of animals

To Learn More

AT THE LIBRARY

Duling, Kaitlyn. *Red Pandas*. Minneapolis, Minn.: Bellwether Media, 2021.

London, Martha. *Red Pandas*. Minnetonka, Minn.: Kaleidoscope Pub., 2019.

Murray, Julie. *Red Pandas*. Minneapolis, Minn.: Abdo, 2023.

ON THE WEB

FACTSURFER

Factsurfer.com gives you a safe, fun way to find more information.

1. Go to www.factsurfer.com.

2. Enter "red pandas" into the search box and click 🔍.

3. Select your book cover to see a list of related content.

Index

The images in this book are reproduced through the courtesy of: Hyserb, front cover, p. 17; Eric Isselee, pp. 3, 23; Ondrej Prosicky, p. 4; Vladislav 3, p. 5; Jane Rix, p. 6; Vibhu Bahl/ Alamy, p. 8; Scott Kemper/ Alamy, p. 9 (top left); tawanroong, p. 9 (top right); Hung Chung Chih, p. 9 (bottom); Daniel Prudek, p. 10; stepko, pp. 10-11; Keitma/ Alamy, p. 12; esdeem, p. 13 (top left); Arek Sangkamanee, p. 13 (top right); 06photo, p. 13 (bottom); Rosanne Tackaberry/ Alamy, p. 14; imageBROKER/ Alamy, p. 15; Michael Verbeek, p. 16; Wenn Rights Ltd/ Alamy, p. 18; Kondoruk, p. 19; Sergey Novikov, p. 20; Edo Schmidt/ Alamy, pp. 20-21.